BLAZERS

PRO WRESTLING GREATS

BY ANN WEIL

Reading Consultant:
Barbara J. Fox
Reading Specialist
North Carolina State University

CAPSTONE PRESS
a capstone imprint

Blazers is published by Capstone Press,
151 Good Counsel Drive, P.O. Box 669, Mankato, Minnesota 56002.
www.capstonepub.com

Library of Congress Cataloging-in-Publication Data
Weil, Ann.
    Pro wrestling greats / by Ann Weil.
    p. cm. — (Blazers. best of the best)
    Includes bibliographical references and index.
    Summary: "Lists and describes the top pro wrestlers of the past and today"—Provided by
publisher.
    ISBN 978-1-4296-6497-4 (library binding)
    ISBN 978-1-4296-7251-1 (paperback)
 1. Wrestling—Juvenile literature. I. Title. II. Series.
GV1195.3.W675 2012
796.8120922—dc22
[B]   2011002475

*The author dedicates this book to Pauline Bigornia Weiss.

Editorial Credits
Mandy Robbins, editor; Kyle Grenz, designer; Eric Manske, production specialist

Photo Credits
AP Images: Chris Carlson, cover (bottom); CORBIS: Duomo/Steven E. Sutton, 24; Getty Images
Inc.: Ethan Miller, cover (top), 4-5, 8, 10-11, Wire Image/KMazur, 12-13, Wire Image/Matt
Jelonek, 6-7; Globe Photos: John Barrett, 16, 23; Newscom: CD1/WENN/Carrie Devorah,
1(bottom), i01/ZUMA Press/Olivier Andrivon, 1(top), 14-15, Splash News/Heather Rousseau,
19, ZUMA Press/Oliver Andrivon, 20, ZUMA Press/Toronta Star/Tyler Anderson, 26-27, ZUMA
Press/UPN-TV/WWF, 28-29

Artistic Effects
Shutterstock: max blain

Printed in the United States of America in Stevens Point, Wisconsin.
062011   006256R

TABLE OF CONTENTS

WHAT MAKES A WRESTLER GREAT?

A great wrestler is one that fans love—or love to hate. Pro wrestlers have strength, skill, and attitude. They use **gimmicks** to excite fans.

gimmick–a clever trick used to get people's attention

HULK HOGAN
(1953-)

Hulk Hogan became a pro wrestling star in the 1980s. His fame led to roles in movies and on TV. In 2005 Hulk Hogan joined the World Wrestling Entertainment (WWE) Hall of Fame.

 In 1985 Hulk Hogan wrestled in the main event for the first WrestleMania. This annual event hosts the biggest wrestling matchups of the year.

TRICKED OUT!

LIONSAULT
to backflip off the middle rope
and land on an opponent

8

CHRIS JERICHO

(1970-)

Chris Jericho crushes other wrestlers with his two **signature moves**. First he flips into a **Lionsault**. Then he defeats them with **The Walls of Jericho**.

THE WALLS OF JERICHO
to turn the opponent facedown and grab both of his legs, bending the back and legs toward the opponent's head

signature move—the move for which a wrestler is best known; this move is also called a finishing move

TRICKED OUT!

ATTITUDE ADJUSTMENT
to lift an opponent into a shoulder carry, then slam him down to the mat

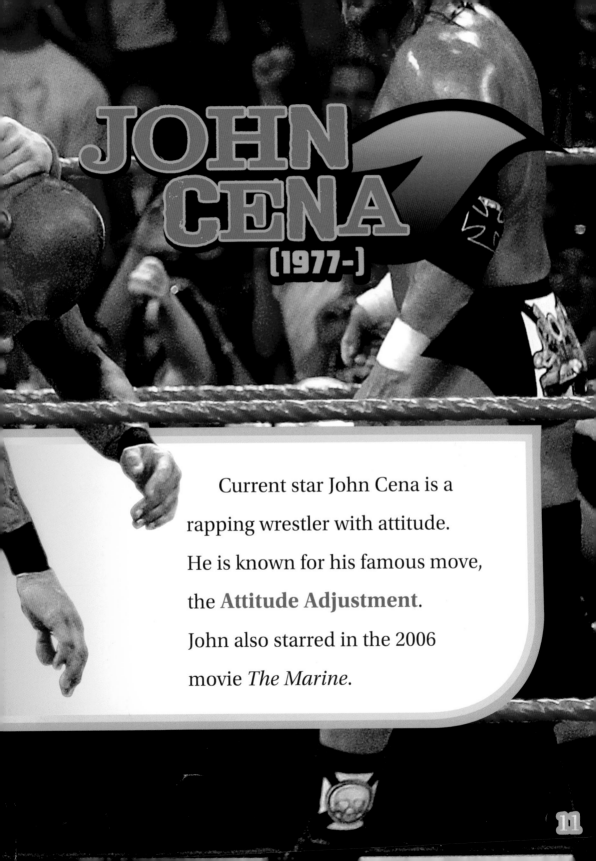

JOHN CENA

(1977-)

Current star John Cena is a rapping wrestler with attitude. He is known for his famous move, the **Attitude Adjustment**. John also starred in the 2006 movie *The Marine*.

MICK FOLEY
(1965-)

Mick Foley shocks fans with his **aggressive** wrestling style. He often uses a baseball bat wrapped in barbed wire.

aggressive–strong and forceful

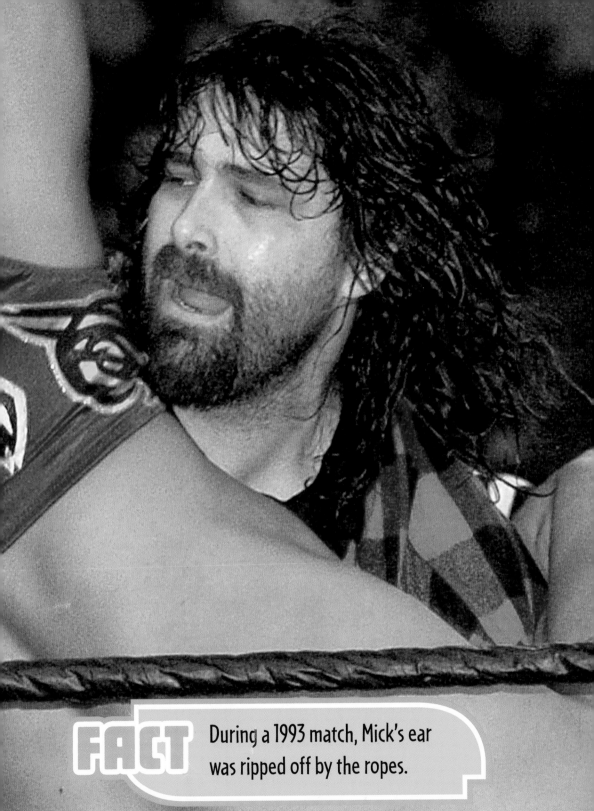

FACT During a 1993 match, Mick's ear was ripped off by the ropes.

MYSTERIO

(1974-)

Rey Mysterio is smaller than most wrestlers. But he is no lightweight. He won the WWE World Heavyweight Championship for the second time in 2010.

FACT

As a child, Rey Mysterio watched his uncle wrestle. He uses his uncle's ring name but spells it differently.

BIG SHOW

(1972-)

Facing Big Show is like staring down a mountain. He is called "The World's Largest Athlete." Big Show is a five-time WWE World Champion.

FACT Big Show is 7 feet (2 meters) tall and weighs around 500 pounds (227 kilograms).

UNDERTAKER

(1965-)

Undertaker's fiery ring entrance has sent wrestlers running. Those who stay risk his **Tombstone Piledriver**.

 Undertaker has never lost his WrestleMania championship title.

TRICKED OUT!

TOMBSTONE PILEDRIVER
to hold an opponent upside down against
the stomach and then drop to the knees

TRICKED OUT!

SWEET CHIN MUSIC
a lightning-fast kick to the chin

SHAWN MICHAELS

(1965-)

Shawn Michaels was the first wrestler to hold four wrestling titles at once. He called himself the Grand Slam Champion. Now any wrestler who holds four titles at once gains that title.

 **FACT** Shawn Michaels' signature move is called Sweet Chin Music.

DWAYNE "THE ROCK" JOHNSON (1972-)

Dwayne "The Rock" Johnson won fans over with his big mouth and bad attitude. The Rock won the WWE World Championship title in 1998.

FACT Dwayne has starred in movies and written a best-selling book.

FACT Stone Cold has won a total of 17 wrestling championships.

"STONE COLD" STEVE AUSTIN

(1964-)

This six-time WWE World Champion never gives up. In 1997 Stone Cold was **paralyzed** for a few minutes after a hard hit. He finished the match and won!

paralyzed–unable to move

E.D.G.E

(1973-)

Edge started out as a **tag team** wrestler with his childhood friend, Christian. Edge won his first individual WWE championship in 2006.

tag team—two or more wrestlers who take turns fighting opponents in a match

FACT In 1997 Triple H formed a wrestling team with Shawn Michaels and Chyna. They called themselves D-Generation X.

TRIPLE H
(1969-)

Triple H is a force in the ring. He has held more WWE titles than any other wrestler. Exciting wrestlers like Triple H keep fans wild about pro wrestling.

GLOSSARY

aggressive (uh-GREH-siv)—strong and forceful

gimmick (GIM-ik)—a clever trick or idea used to get people's attention

paralyzed (PAIR-uh-lized)—unable to move or feel

signature move (SIG-nuh-chur MOOV)—the move for which a wrestler is best known; this move is also called a finishing move

tag team (TAG TEEM)—two or more wrestlers who take turns fighting their opponents in a match

title (TYE-tuhl)—a championship

READ MORE

O'Shei, Tim. *Undertaker.* Stars of Pro Wrestling. Mankato, Minn.: Capstone Press, 2010.

Price, Sean. *The Kids' Guide to Pro Wrestling.* Kids' Guides. Mankato, Minn.: Capstone Press, 2012.

Shields, Brian. *Triple H.* DK Readers. London: New York: DK Publishing, 2009.

INTERNET SITES

FactHound offers a safe, fun way to find Internet sites related to this book. All of the sites on FactHound have been researched by our staff.

Here's all you do:

Visit *www.facthound.com*

Type in this code: 9781429664974

Super-cool stuff!

Check out projects, games and lots more at
www.capstonekids.com

INDEX

I'm a Little Teapot
and Other Movement Songs

Illustrated by
Anne Kennedy

Cartwheel
·B·O·O·K·S· ™

SCHOLASTIC INC.
NEW YORK TORONTO LONDON AUCKLAND SYDNEY

For Jack
— A.K.

ISBN 0-590-47275-5

Copyright © 1994 by Scholastic Inc.
Illustrations copyright © 1994 by Anne Kennedy.
CARTWHEEL BOOKS is a registered trademark of Scholastic Inc.
All rights reserved. Published by Scholastic Inc.

12 11 10 9 8 7 6 5 4 3   4 5 6 7 8 9/9

Printed in the U.S.A.   24

First Scholastic printing, March 1994

Contents

I'm a Little Teapot

I'm a little teapot, short and stout;

Here is my handle, here is my spout.

When I get all steamed up, then I shout;
Just tip me over and pour me out!

The Mulberry Bush

Here we go round the mulberry bush,
The mulberry bush, the mulberry bush.
Here we go round the mulberry bush,
So early in the morning.

This is the way we wash our face,
Wash our face, wash our face.
This is the way we wash our face,
So early in the morning.

This is the way we brush our teeth,
Brush our teeth, brush our teeth.
This is the way we brush our teeth,
So early in the morning.

This is the way we comb our hair,
Comb our hair, comb our hair.
This is the way we comb our hair,
So early in the morning.

This is the way we button our clothes,
Button our clothes, button our clothes.
This is the way we button our clothes,
So early in the morning.

This is the way we go to school,
Go to school, go to school.
This is the way we go to school,
So early in the morning.

Here we go round the mulberry bush,
The mulberry bush, the mulberry bush.
Here we go round the mulberry bush,
So early in the morning.

The Itsy, Bitsy Spider

The itsy, bitsy spider went up the water spout.
Down came the rain and washed the spider out.
Out came the sun and dried up all the rain,
And the itsy, bitsy spider went up the spout again.

The Farmer in the Dell

The farmer in the dell,
The farmer in the dell,
Heigh-ho, the derry-o,
The farmer in the dell.

The farmer takes a wife,
The farmer takes a wife,
Heigh-ho, the derry-o,
The farmer takes a wife.

The wife takes a child,
The wife takes a child,
Heigh-ho, the derry-o,
The wife takes a child.

The child takes a nurse,
The child takes a nurse,
Heigh-ho, the derry-o,
The child takes a nurse.

The nurse takes a dog,
The nurse takes a dog,
Heigh-ho, the derry-o,
The nurse takes a dog.

The dog takes a cat,
The dog takes a cat,
Heigh-ho, the derry-o,
The dog takes a cat.

The cat takes a rat,
The cat takes a rat,
Heigh-ho, the derry-o,
The cat takes a rat.

The rat takes the cheese,
The rat takes the cheese,
Heigh-ho, the derry-o,
The rat takes the cheese.

The cheese stands alone,
The cheese stands alone,
Heigh-ho, the derry-o,
The cheese stands alone.

Brown Girl in the Ring

There's a brown girl in the ring,
Tra la la la la;
There's a brown girl in the ring,
Tra la la la;
There's a brown girl in the ring,
Tra la la la la;
For she likes sugar and I like plums.

First you skip across the ocean,
Tra la la la la;
First you skip across the ocean,
Tra la la la;
First you skip across the ocean,
Tra la la la la;
For she likes sugar and I like plums.

Then you show me your motion,
Tra la la la la;
Then you show me your motion,
Tra la la la;
Then you show me your motion,
Tra la la la la;
For she likes sugar and I like plums.

Then you wheel and take a partner,
Tra la la la la;
Then you wheel and take a partner,
Tra la la la;
Then you wheel and take a partner,
Tra la la la la;
For she likes sugar and I like plums.

The Hokey Pokey

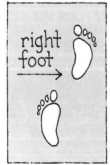

You put your right foot in,
You put your right foot out,
You put your right foot in,
And you shake it all about.
You do the hokey pokey,
And you turn yourself around,
That's what it's all about!

You put your left foot in,
You put your left foot out,

left foot

You put your left foot in,
And you shake it all about.
You do the hokey pokey,
And you turn yourself around,
That's what it's all about!

You put your right hand in,
You put your right hand out,
You put your right hand in,
And you shake it all about.
You do the hokey pokey,
And you turn yourself around,
That's what it's all about!

right
hand

You put your left hand in,
You put your left hand out,
You put your left hand in,
And you shake it all about.
You do the hokey pokey,
And you turn yourself around,
That's what it's all about!

left
hand

You put your right hip in,
You put your right hip out,
You put your right hip in,
And you shake it all about.
You do the hokey pokey,
And you turn yourself around,
That's what it's all about!

You put your left hip in,
You put your left hip out,
You put your left hip in,
And you shake it all about.
You do the hokey pokey,
And you turn yourself around,
That's what it's all about!

You put your whole self in,
You put your whole self out,
You put your whole self in,
And you shake yourself about.
You do the hokey pokey,
And you turn yourself around,
That's what it's all about!

If You're Happy and You Know It

If you're happy and you know it, clap your hands.
If you're happy and you know it, clap your hands.
If you're happy and you know it,
And you really want to show it,
If you're happy and you know it, clap your hands.

If you're happy and you know it, stomp your feet.
If you're happy and you know it, stomp your feet.
If you're happy and you know it,
And you really want to show it,
If you're happy and you know it, stomp your feet.

27

If you're happy and you know it, shout "Hurray!"
If you're happy and you know it, shout "Hurray!"
If you're happy and you know it,
And you really want to show it,
If you're happy and you know it, shout "Hurray!"

28

If you're happy and you know it, do all three.
If you're happy and you know it, do all three.
If you're happy and you know it,
And you really want to show it,
If you're happy and you know it, do all three.
Clap your hands! Stomp your feet! Shout "Hurray!"

Teddy Bear, Teddy Bear

Teddy Bear, Teddy Bear,
Turn around.

Teddy Bear, Teddy Bear,
Touch the ground.

Teddy Bear, Teddy Bear,
Show your shoe.

Teddy Bear, Teddy Bear,
That will do!

Teddy Bear, Teddy Bear,
Hands on head.

Teddy Bear, Teddy Bear,
Go to bed.

Teddy Bear, Teddy Bear,
March upstairs.

Teddy Bear, Teddy Bear,
Say your prayers.

Teddy Bear, Teddy Bear,
Turn off the light.
Teddy Bear, Teddy Bear,
Say good night!